Alive in the WORD

CLOUD OF WITNESSES

MOSES

Called and Equipped

Catherine Upchurch

Little Rock Scripture Study

A ministry of the Diocese of Little Rock
in partnership with Liturgical Press

Nihil obstat: Jerome Kodell, O.S.B., *Censor Librorum.*
Imprimatur: ✠ Anthony B. Taylor, Bishop of Little Rock, July 21, 2016.

Cover design by Ann Blattner. Cover photo: Thinkstock Images by Getty. Used with permission.

Photos/illustrations: Pages 6 (burning bush), 9 (slaves in Egypt), 11, 13 (top and bottom), 17, 21, 23 (pharaoh), and 27, Thinkstock Images by Getty. Used with permission. Page 35, *The Brazen Serpent* by James Tissot, Brooklyn Museum, Brooklyn, New York. Courtesy of Wikimedia Commons. Page 42, map from *Little Rock Catholic Study Bible*, created by Robert Cronan of Lucidity Information Design, LLC © 2011 Little Rock Scripture Study. Used with permission.

ISBN: 978-0-8146-3699-2 (print); 978-0-8146-4673-1 (ebook)

Contents

Introduction

Alive in the Word brings you resources to deepen your understanding of Scripture, offer meaning for your life today, and help you to pray and act in response to God's word.

Use any volume of **Alive in the Word** in the way best suited to you.

- **For individual learning and reflection,** consider this an invitation to prayerfully journal in response to the questions you find along the way. And be prepared to move from head to heart and then to action.
- **For group learning and reflection,** arrange for three sessions where you will use the material provided as the basis for faith sharing and prayer. You may ask group members to read each chapter in advance and come prepared with questions answered. In this kind of session, plan to be together for about an hour. Or, if your group prefers, read and respond to the questions together without advance preparation. With this approach, it's helpful to plan on spending more time for each group session in order to adequately work through each chapter.

- **For a parish-wide event** or use within a larger group, provide each person with a copy of this volume, and allow time during the event for quiet reading, group discussion, and prayer, and then a final commitment by each person to some simple action in response to what he or she learned.

This volume exploring the life of Moses is one of several volumes dedicated to the **Cloud of Witnesses** theme. The pages of our Bibles are filled with the stories of women and men who have played a unique role in salvation history. By entering into a few key biblical passages written by or describing these people, we begin to see how our own story continues God's great work of salvation in the world. Their witness, handed on to us from centuries ago, continues to speak to us and challenge us to stand as faithful witnesses in today's world.

The Burning Bush

Begin by asking God to assist you in your prayer and study. Then slowly read through Exodus 2:23b–3:6, which describes Moses and his burning bush experience. The fact that this is a familiar scene alerts us to the need to hear it in a fresh way.

Exodus 2:23b–3:6

[2:23]The Israelites groaned under their bondage and cried out, and from their bondage their cry for help went up to God. [24]God heard their moaning and God was mindful of his covenant with Abraham, Isaac and Jacob. [25]God saw the Israelites, and God knew. . . .

[3:1]Meanwhile Moses was tending the flock of his father-in-law Jethro, the priest of Midian. Leading the flock beyond the wilderness, he came to the mountain of God, Horeb. [2]There the angel of the LORD appeared to him as fire flaming out of a bush. When he looked, although the bush was on fire, it was not being consumed. [3]So Moses decided, "I must turn aside to look at this remarkable sight. Why does the bush not burn up?" [4]When the LORD saw that he had turned aside to look, God called out to him from the bush: Moses! Moses!

He answered, "Here I am." [5]God said: Do not come near! Remove your sandals from your feet, for the place where you stand is holy ground. [6]I am the God of your father, he continued, the God of Abraham, the God of Isaac, and the God of Jacob. Moses hid his face, for he was afraid to look at God.

After a few moments of quiet reflection on Exodus 2:23b–3:6, consider the following background information in "Setting the Scene."

Setting the Scene

How did it come to be that Israel was in bondage? The final chapters of Genesis tell of Jacob and his children and grandchildren who traveled from the land of Canaan to Egypt in order to escape famine. Their large families settled there, remained there over generations, and multiplied. These descendants are sometimes referred to as Hebrews and sometimes as Israelites, since they are descendants of Jacob, whose name was changed to Israel after encountering God (Gen 32:23-31).

In time, in a story that unfolds in the first two chapters of Exodus, Egypt's pharaoh (also referred to as a king) became convinced that the growth of the Israelites would threaten the stability of Egypt, and so he issued a mandate to impose hard labor, which soon became slavery. Rather than diminish the size of these descendant tribal families, their growth continued, so much so that Pharaoh decreed the slaughter of the male children of the Hebrew slaves. Moses, however, the child of slaves, escaped this fate when the midwives spared his life and his mother wisely hid him among the reeds of the Nile River, where he was discovered by Pharaoh's daughter and raised in her household.

Pharaoh's daughter is an unexpected deliverer in this scene. When has an apparent outsider come to the rescue of someone you love? Or when has an outsider provided the needed solution in a situation?

It was Pharaoh's daughter who named the child *Moses*, an Egyptian name akin to the Hebrew word that means "I drew him out" of the water, perhaps a foreshadowing of what would come for all of God's people. It was God who would provide a way through the waters when the Hebrews were later escaping Egypt (Exod 14:15-22), and in the New Testament it is God who will invite his people to enter the waters of baptism to be drawn out into new life. This singular story of Pharaoh's daughter offering "salvation" to a helpless child provides an opening act to the great drama of God's full gift of salvation in the offering of his Son, who was anything but helpless.

One final note will set the scene. By the end of the second chapter of Exodus we encounter a fully adult Moses who is tending sheep for his father-in-law. The action has shifted away from the Nile Delta of Egypt and into the wilderness of the region known as Midian, perhaps at this ancient time to be found in the Sinai Peninsula. (See the map on page 42.) Moses had struck and killed an Egyptian taskmaster for abusing one of the Hebrew slaves (Exod 2:11-15), so he fled to avoid capital punishment, settled in the region of Midian, and assumed what he surely hoped would be a very ordinary life.

Understanding the Scene Itself

The entire passage from Exodus will be considered a few verses at a time. The occasional questions in the margin (as above) are for discussion with others. If you are using these materials on your own, use the questions for personal reflection or as a guide to journaling.

**2:23The Israelites groaned under their bondage
and cried out, and from their bondage their cry
for help went up to God. 24God heard their
moaning and God was mindful of his covenant
with Abraham, Isaac and Jacob. 25God saw the
Israelites, and God knew. . . .**

At the start of the book of Exodus, we are told that the slaves led a "bitter" life and were forced to build the garrison cities of Pithom and Raamses by mortar and brick and all kinds of field work (1:11-14). Their bondage could not prevent them from groaning and crying out, which became the opening for God to begin to act. Their groans articulated their need and opened the way for divine intervention. Divine action begins with mindfulness and involves hearing, seeing, and knowing.

What does it mean to say that God was mindful of his covenant? Did God need a reminder? Had God temporarily forgotten the covenant bond with Abraham and his descendants who were now in slavery? Was God so distracted so as not to notice that these people were cruelly oppressed? Was the Psalm writer wrong when he proclaimed "[The Lord] remembers forever his covenant, / the word he commended for a thousand generations" (Ps 105:8)?

To say that God was mindful of the covenant, or remembered the covenant, should not imply that somehow God had forgotten. The Hebrew word translated as "mindful" or "remembered" actually conveys the idea of acting *because of* remembrance. In other words, God takes seriously the covenant obligation and is ready to take action, zealously committing himself to the cause of this suffering people. God's hearing, seeing, and knowing is a personal investment; it is evidence of intimacy. God does not just observe from afar but suffers with this oppressed people and ensures that they will be delivered through divine action. The stage is set for how God will work.

In what situations does it seem that God seems to be missing? How have you been called to trust that God will indeed act? What tests this belief for you?

3:1 Meanwhile Moses was tending the flock of his father-in-law Jethro, the priest of Midian. Leading the flock beyond the wilderness, he came to the mountain of God, Horeb.

It seems that shepherds appear all along the way in the Bible's story of salvation history. Moses is one of the biblical characters depicted with this job; others include Rachel (Gen 29:9), Jacob (Gen 47:1-3), and David (1 Sam 16:4-13). God is called by the psalmist the Good Shepherd

(Ps 23), and Jesus uses the same phrase when describing himself (John 10:14). Shepherding is an ancient and necessary profession that put food on the table (literally), but it carried a negative stigma as well. The animals themselves were dirty and untrainable. It was demanding work to keep a herd together, to find sources of water in an arid landscape, and to provide protection from wild animals and the severe temperatures of a desert climate. The demands of daily care of animals that needed land in which to roam made it a rather solitary undertaking.

But Moses was fortunate to have an occupation and a family. Upon fleeing Egypt to avoid prosecution and certain death for his crime of killing an Egyptian overlord, he settled in the region of Midian, met the daughters of the local priest there, helped them water their flock, and soon found himself welcomed and wed. The needs of his father-in-law's sheep took Moses into the wilderness where he would encounter God at Mount Horeb—sometimes assumed to be the same as Mount Sinai and sometimes designated in another location. The verse is written in a way that describes Horeb as "the mountain of God," but this would seem to be a reflection on what happened next in the story rather than a description of an already well-known place of encounter. Did Moses go there

intending this encounter? Certainly not, as we see in the following verses.

[2]There the angel of the Lord appeared to him as fire flaming out of a bush. When he looked, although the bush was on fire, it was not being consumed. [3]So Moses decided, "I must turn aside to look at this remarkable sight. Why does the bush not burn up?" [4]When the Lord saw that he had turned aside to look, God called out to him from the bush: Moses! Moses! He answered, "Here I am."

When have you become aware that God has been trying to get your attention? How did this become apparent to you? If you feel you are still waiting for God to use some kind of burning bush to reach you, what might you need to do in order to be more open or attentive?

One rabbinical tradition suggests that Moses had passed that bush—and, thereby, the voice of God—many times, until finally God set the bush on fire to get his attention! Another tradition proposes that it was on fire for quite some time and not consumed, just waiting for Moses to finally be free enough of his own limited vision and agenda to notice something bigger and brighter. These are humorous and even insightful ways to ponder the significance of that experience that we associate so strongly with the call of Moses.

The instigator of the encounter is God—"the angel of the Lord appeared to him as fire flaming out of a bush." The instrument is fire. In this scene, the natural world becomes the vehicle for delivering the supernatural. And this will be a continuing theme throughout Scripture. While the flames surely capture Moses' attention, we will soon understand that God wants more than just his attention; God wants Moses' commitment to something beyond that moment in the desert.

In this story it was God who first saw and heard and now it is Moses who sees (the flaming bush) and hears (his name). At the sound of his name he responds as if reporting for duty: "Here I am." In the original Hebrew of this story, this phrase "Here I am" translates one word—*hineni*—and conveys the sense of readiness.

5God said: Do not come near! Remove your sandals from your feet, for the place where you stand is holy ground. 6I am the God of your father, he continued, the God of Abraham, the God of Isaac, and the God of Jacob. Moses hid his face, for he was afraid to look at God.

In these two verses we discover something about the awesome mystery that is God. This God is familiar and close, the God of the ancestors whose names and stories are remembered. At the same time this God is totally other and distinct from human experience. Moses is warned not to come near, and we are told that he is afraid to look at God. Later, in Exodus 33:7-23, we learn of the tent of meeting that

It is possible that we glimpse God's face in the ordinary or routine aspects of our lives and that as we grow in our capacity to do this, we grow closer to God. In what ways, or in what relationships, have you caught a glimpse of God's face from time to time? How might you allow these moments of recognition to shape your capacity to recognize God more and more?

The novelist Joseph Heller is credited with this insight: Moses took off his shoes and "there went the rest of his life!" When has an awareness of God's real presence affected you or someone you know in such a way that some aspect of life changes as well?

Moses set up just outside the camp of the Israelites. Here we are told that God and Moses would meet "face to face, as a person speaks to a friend" (v. 11). This is an intimate relationship, and yet just a few verses later when Moses pleads with God to see his glory we are told that the Lord reminded Moses that "no one can see me and live" (v. 20).

These apparently contradictory verses offer some evidence that at least two traditions from the ancient Israelites have been preserved and woven together. It creates a real tension in the text, and perhaps that tension is indeed what we must ponder from this inspired text. God is both close at hand and totally beyond our reach. We may wonder whether this also has something to do with our capacity to know God truly and fully, a capacity that hopefully grows throughout our lives as believers.

Moses removes his sandals in recognition of the holy. What makes the place holy, as mentioned earlier, is not that it was already a designated religious site. Rather, its holiness, its character as set apart by God, is the result of this encounter. This encounter will lead to a relationship between Moses and God that is marked by struggle, trust, responsibility, reverence, and courage. Like so many relationships, it is in the nitty-gritty that we discover who we are for each other.

Praying the Word / Sacred Reading

The words of prayer below tap into the almost-too-good-to-be-true message that the God who sought out Moses also seeks us and is prepared to set bushes on fire to capture our attention and call us into relationship. Feel free to add your own words—what you hear that God dares us to believe. Pause in quiet listening between each refrain.

O God, you dare us to believe that bushes on
fire will not be consumed
and that you know us well enough to call out
our names.
Can it be?
I come before you admitting my doubts
and hoping my eyes and ears will direct me
where my mind and will initially hesitate
to go.

O God, you dare us to believe that even dirt
can be sanctified by your presence
and that the holy can be evident in the ordinary.
Can it be?
Allow my feet to walk upon this earth
in a way that acknowledges your presence
and places me before you in humility.

O God, you dare us to believe that the master
of the universe
hears the cry of the oppressed.
Can it be?
When injustice demands a response
teach me to present to you the needs
of those whose voices may be silenced
by abuse.

Living the Word

In the midst of ordinary duties of his day, Moses followed his curiosity and made time to examine the world right around him. His investment led to an encounter that changed his life and the life of many others. Although we may not experience a literal burning bush or a change so radical that we are aware of its effects in our lives, are we open to considering how God may be trying to catch our attention? Are we willing to still ourselves long enough to recognize the holy in our midst? Consider these suggestions that might create in us the capacity to "take off our sandals" in God's presence:

- Invite God to speak to you in the course of your day. Be deliberate in creating this opening in your heart.
- Ask God to create in you what might be called a "holy curiosity"—not just to seek out what is novel but an eagerness to explore God's presence in new ways.
- Identify what, in hindsight, might be a burning bush or two in your life. When have you had a sense that God sent you in a new direction? How did this occur? Recognizing such events in your personal history may help to heighten your awareness of how and when God may be calling you or acting through you in the future.

Moses Is Commissioned

Begin by asking God to assist you in your prayer and study. Then slowly read through Exodus 3:7-10, which describes God's plan for the enslaved and for Moses.

Exodus 3:7-10

**7 But the LORD said: I have wit-
nessed the affliction of my
people in Egypt and have
heard their cry against their
taskmasters, so I know well what they are suffering. 8 There-
fore I have come down to rescue them from the power of the
Egyptians and lead them up from that land into a good and
spacious land, a land flowing with milk and honey, the coun-
try of the Canaanites, the Hittites, the Amorites, the Perizzites,
the Girgashites, the Hivites and the Jebusites. 9 Now indeed
the outcry of the Israelites has reached me, and I have seen
how the Egyptians are oppressing them. 10 Now, go! I am
sending you to Pharaoh to bring my people, the Israelites, out
of Egypt.**

After a few moments of quiet reflection on the commission of Moses, consider the information in "Setting the Scene."

Setting the Scene

In spite of Moses' previous awe and fear of looking at God, events are about to take a surprising turn. God has other plans. God wants to do more than simply grab attention or wow this simple shepherd. God's words will draw Moses into relationship—a relationship with benefits and responsibilities as we will soon discover.

These verses contain the first words attributed to God in the book of Exodus, the most crucial story of Israel's self-understanding. They are addressed to Moses in this dramatic scene but, in addition, they are addressed to those who are oppressed in Egypt and to those oppressed in all generations. These words reveal the kind of God who will always be the principal actor in the story of salvation, a God who acts on behalf of those who are on the edges of society, whose voices often go unheard, and whose basic human dignity demands a response.

The God we worship is the God who hears the cry of the poor and saves those whose spirits are crushed (see Ps 34). The words of God to Moses in Exodus 3:7-10, the actions of God on behalf of the enslaved in Egypt, are embodied in the life of Jesus and become the standard by which we evaluate our own covenant relationship with God. The United States Conference of Catholic Bishops, in its document *Communities of Salt and Light*, states the following:

> Parishes are called to reach out to the hurting, the poor, and the vulnerable in our midst in concrete acts of charity. Just as the gospel tells us our lives will be judged by our response to the "least of these" so too our parishes should be measured by our help for the hungry, the homeless, the troubled and the alienated—in our own community and beyond.

What parish activities are you aware of that extend God's loving care to those in most need? How is your faith community made aware of the need that is present in your midst?

Indeed, while the story of God and Moses at the burning bush comes from a time and place very removed from our own time and place, its lessons continue to animate what it means to know God and to love God and neighbor.

Understanding the Scene Itself

Each verse from Exodus 3:7-10 will be considered a few verses at a time. The occasional questions in the margin (as above) may be used for discussion with others, or for your personal reflection.

7But the LORD said: I have witnessed the affliction of my people in Egypt and have heard their cry against their taskmasters, so I know well what they are suffering.

Already, before those enslaved in Egypt have even been introduced to God's plan for their liberation, God is referring to them as "my people." The bond of relationship emerges in the very language of God, a bond that will be further demonstrated in the actions God will take on behalf of the slaves. This God is far from indifferent. This God is fully aware of their plight and takes action.

Verse 7 makes use of three verbs to express God's level of engagement: witnessed, heard, and know well. These verbs indicate a growing intimacy between the people and the God known before only through ancestral stories. In this context, witnessing means more than simply observing or taking note from a distance. God witnesses in a way that carries what is seen into his very being; God hears in a way that moves to an intimate knowing of their situation. "I know well what they are suffering" is an indication that God has compassion, that God actually bears their suffering with them. It is this compassion that will lead to divine action on their behalf.

Compassion is to suffer what others suffer, to enter into their pain with the desire to alleviate it.

8Therefore I have come down to rescue them from the power of the Egyptians and lead them up from that land into a good and spacious land, a land flowing with milk and honey, the country of the Canaanites, the Hittites, the Amorites, the Perizzites, the Girgashites, the Hivites and the Jebusites.

The feeling of compassion is converted to the action required by compassion. God is portrayed as coming down in order to lead the oppressed up. This "downward" movement of God toward the human condition has a purpose: to liberate the oppressed, to bring them "up" so that they are not defined or restricted by the circumstances that limit their self-understanding or their understanding of God. Those enslaved in Egypt were bound to serve Pharaoh and his narrow purposes. They were stuck in the repetition of meaningless labor and lack of dignity. God's intervention, portrayed here as coming down, is meant to rescue them not just from the conditions of physical slavery but from the emotional and mental slavery that surely went along with generations of oppression.

The land where God will lead the people is described as "good and spacious," "flowing with milk and honey." An unbiased look at the land they would enter, the land of Canaan later to be known as Israel, might question this lyrical description. The people who come as pilgrims escaping persecution have traveled through the rocky mountainous terrain of the Sinai Peninsula. (See map on p. 42.) And even though some of Joshua's men will scout the land on the other side of the Jordan River and come back reportedly carrying gigantic grapes and pomegranates and figs (see Num 13:21-24), the geography has not in fact changed that much. However, there is a small river, the Jordan, and in a rocky desert, even a small river can provide a measure of fertility and the promise of abundance.

This pattern of God coming down and raising up is also captured by St. Paul. In the hymn found in Philippians 2:5-11, it is Christ Jesus who humbles himself by taking on flesh and even dying on a cross, and it is Christ who is then greatly exalted. Paul urges the followers of Jesus to have the same attitude, to be willing to surrender ourselves to God. How can such surrender be experienced as liberating? What experiences help you to understand the value of serving the God who will become humble on our behalf?

Think of a time when you believe God was giving you a new start. What words would you use to express this new reality?

Surely the land "flowing with milk and honey" is meant to suggest more than a change of scenery. Could it also evoke a sense of promise for a new life that will be less nomadic and more secure? A life that will be rooted in God's promise to accompany his people? The abundance suggested by milk and honey is as much about the rich promise of freedom as it is about establishing a place to call home.

The listing of all the various peoples who populate the land where God will lead them is a reminder that the land already has occupants. It will not be a simple entry into the land. In fact, the eventual entry of God's people into Canaan is described as a military conquest (see the book of Joshua, especially 21:43-45, or a more graphic description in Deut 20:16-18). Bear in mind that this was a time when power was often associated with the victory that could be assigned to various gods. The God revealed to Moses and to those who escape slavery proves his power in victory.

9Now indeed the outcry of the Israelites has reached me, and I have seen how the Egyptians are oppressing them. 10Now, go! I am sending you to Pharaoh to bring my people, the Israelites, out of Egypt.

God's compassion and intervention now rests squarely on Moses, who is commissioned to act as God's instrument in freeing the Hebrews enslaved in Egypt. We can only imagine the gut responses that pulsed through Moses: he was a wanted man who was being sent back to the scene of his crime.

- He was a "nobody" being sent to address the great Pharaoh of Egypt.
- He was in the presence of God and God wanted his service.

God does not pose a question to Moses such as "Will you go for me?" Instead, God—who calls Moses by name and knows him as he knows his own people—simply says "Go!" In one sentence Moses is given his marching orders. Apparently we, along with Moses himself, are asked to believe that he is capable of mediating the release of God's people. But his capability is God's doing and not his own. This same pattern of God calling those who seem unqualified, or using for divine purposes those who seem very unlikely, appears throughout Scripture. As examples, consider:

- Abraham and Sarah were so elderly that they knew their childbearing years were behind them (Gen 12:1-4; 17:6-8), and yet God chose them to build up a great nation with numerous descendants.
- David, known throughout history as Israel's ideal king, was the youngest child of a family of shepherds (1 Sam 16:4-13). He did not come from a royal family and had no

training in the demands of political and military leadership.

- Amos was a herdsman and dresser of sycamores before God called him to prophesy to his people (Amos 7:14-15). He was not anxious to be a prophet and we have no evidence that he was schooled in such a task.
- Rahab, a known prostitute in Jericho, surely would have been an unlikely tool for God to use, and yet she offered protection for Joshua's soldiers as they planned to enter Canaan (Josh 2:1-24).
- Matthew was probably not the most obvious choice for a disciple. As a tax collector who worked for the Roman occupiers of Israel, he would hardly have been considered trustworthy, and yet Jesus chose him to be a follower and then to preach the Good News (Matt 9:9-10; 10:3).
- Paul (also known as Saul), the great evangelist to the Gentile world, certainly would not have seemed a likely choice to preach the Gospel. His background as an avid Pharisee who was commissioned to rid Judaism of the followers of Jesus would seem to disqualify him, but God thought otherwise (Acts 8:1-3; 9:1-19).

Can you think of other examples where it seemed God used an unlikely person to accomplish some purpose in our world? Could you be that unlikely person?

Praying the Word / Sacred Reading

Use your imagination to place yourself before God. Perhaps light a candle as a reminder of the flames that captured Moses' attention at the burning bush. After a few moments of silence ask God to help you see what pains and sorrows are the concerns of his heart. What oppression does God see and know and embrace? What people might God want to raise up and even figuratively lead to a promised land?

After some time of simply sitting and envisioning the various scenes and people in our world, pray with words of your own or using those that follow:

In the midst of plenty there are people who
have so little.
In the midst of joy there are those whose
sorrow is raw.
In the midst of blessing there is sometimes
suffering and oppression.

O God of burning bushes and holy ground,
I come before you and ask for the courage
to see and hear as you do,
To leave behind my fear and place myself in
a position to hear you call my name.

Living the Word

Here are some ideas to bring flesh to the words of God commissioning Moses for his great task:

- Talk with your parish staff or parish council about the needs that are present in your own neighborhood that the parish might be able to address in some way.
  - Are there elderly or ill people who might need help with household chores?
  - Are there civic issues involving workers that might provide an opportunity for learning within the parish?
  - Is there some group within the parish that is currently trying to address justice issues in the area? Could they be provided an opportunity to address the larger parish and get more people involved in their efforts?
- In the ritual of baptism, we are each called by name to enter into the death and resurrection of Jesus, to embrace the faith that our Catholic community professes, and by implication to serve God and God's people. What gifts or talents do you bring to share with the faith community? Could this be your response to Gods' call?

Moses Hesitates and God Equips

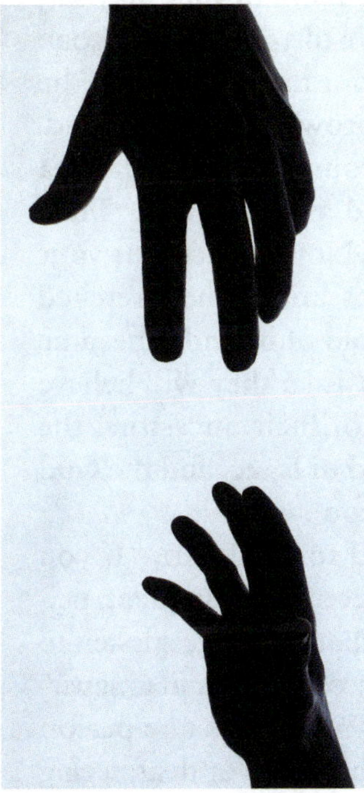

Begin by asking God to assist you in your prayer and study as you slowly read through sections of Exodus 3:11–4:17. These verses depict the internal struggle of Moses to respond to God's call.

Exodus 3:11–4:17 (portions)
3:11But Moses said to God, "Who am
I that I should go to Pharaoh and
bring the Israelites out of Egypt?"
12God answered: I will be with you;
and this will be your sign that I have
sent you. When you have brought
the people out of Egypt, you will
serve God at this mountain. 13"But,"
said Moses to God, "if I go to the
Israelites and say to them, 'The God
of your ancestors has sent me to you,' and they ask me, 'What
is his name?' what do I tell them?" 14God replied to Moses: I
am who I am. Then he added: This is what you will tell the
Israelites: I AM has sent me to you. . . .

18They will listen to you. Then you and the elders of Israel
will go to the king of Egypt and say to him: The LORD, the
God of the Hebrews, has come to meet us. So now, let us go
a three days' journey in the wilderness to offer sacrifice to
the LORD, our God. 19Yet I know that the king of Egypt will

not allow you to go unless his hand is forced. [20]So I will stretch out my hand and strike Egypt with all the wondrous deeds I will do in its midst. After that he will let you go. . . .

[4:1]"But," objected Moses, "suppose they do not believe me or listen to me? For they may say, 'The LORD did not appear to you.' " [2]The LORD said to him: What is in your hand? "A staff," he answered. [3]God said: Throw it on the ground. So he threw it on the ground and it became a snake, and Moses backed away from it. [4]Then the LORD said to Moses: Now stretch out your hand and take hold of its tail. So he stretched out his hand and took hold of it, and it became a staff in his hand. [5]That is so they will believe that the LORD, the God of their ancestors, the God of Abraham, the God of Isaac, and the God of Jacob, did appear to you . . .

[10]Moses, however, said to the LORD, "If you please, my Lord, I have never been eloquent, neither in the past nor now that you have spoken to your servant; but I am slow of speech and tongue." [11]The LORD said to him: Who gives one person speech? Who makes another mute or deaf, seeing or blind? Is it not I, the LORD? [12]Now go, I will assist you in speaking and teach you what you are to say. [13]But he said, "If you please, my Lord, send someone else!" [14]Then the LORD became angry with Moses and said: I know there is your brother, Aaron the Levite, who is a good speaker; even now he is on his way to meet you. When he sees you, he will truly be glad. [15]You will speak to him and put the words in his mouth. I will assist both you and him in speaking and teach you both what you

are to do. [16]He will speak to the people for you: he will be your spokesman, and you will be as God to him. [17]Take this staff in your hand; with it you are to perform the signs.

After a few moments of quiet consideration of the text from Exodus, review what is offered in "Setting the Scene."

Setting the Scene

Now the scene has shifted to Moses and to his struggle to embrace his call. Just by way of background, it is helpful to note that many stories of divine callings in our Bibles also include hesitations and objections from those who are called. In fact, there are several stories in the Old Testament that share a similar pattern when recounting these events. The pattern and elements make up what scholars refer to as a "call narrative." Each of the narratives includes all or some of these elements:

- an encounter with God that makes a strong impression;
- an introductory speech identifying God;
- personal objections to the call, sometimes expressing fear; and
- reassurances from God, often with an accompanying sign.

These elements are present in the story of the call of Moses, and they may also be found in the call of Gideon (Judg 6), the call of Samuel (1 Sam 3), the call of Isaiah (Isa 6), the call of Jeremiah (Jer 1), and the call of Ezekiel (Ezek 1–3). The purpose of using such a pattern in biblical storytelling is not to discount in any way the personal nature of each call. Its use is meant to heighten the divine purpose of leadership among God's people, as well as illustrate an overarching and unified plan of God.

How do you discern, sort out, or wrestle with God's direction in your life? What "tools" do you use?

It might also be helpful to consider that the typical person in biblical times (or even in our own time, for that matter) would naturally wrestle with whether God is indeed calling, how to respond, and what might be possible. These call narratives capture this very human response, but they do so in a way that assures future generations that they are not alone in their struggle and that in the end God will make the "yes" response possible.

In the verses from chapters three and four of Exodus, Moses does not object just once but *five* times: "but" (3:11), "but" (3:13), "but" (4:1), "however" (4:10), and "but" (4:13). We focus our attention on each of these objections and God's response.

Understanding the Scene Itself

> *Each verse selected from Exodus 3–4 will be considered a few verses at a time. The occasional questions in the margin (as above) may be used for discussion with others or for your personal reflection.*

11But Moses said to God, "Who am I that I should go to Pharaoh and bring the Israelites out of Egypt?" 12God answered: I will be with

you; and this will be your sign that I have sent you. When you have brought the people out of Egypt, you will serve God at this mountain.

Moses first objects by indicating that he does not feel worthy, "Who am I that I should go to Pharaoh?" Perhaps God could have chosen someone to approach the king of Egypt who was more obviously qualified or held in high esteem by others. In our own culture, we often associate worthiness with personal accomplishment or abilities, accumulation of goods or fortune, or even natural leadership skills. By those standards, Moses is not worthy. He is a Hebrew by birth and therefore a member of the minority class even though raised by an Egyptian princess, a criminal in the eyes of Egypt's laws, and a shepherd—hardly the chiseled movie star in so many cinematic portraits.

The fact that God responds tells us that Moses is being taken seriously, but God's response doesn't seem to even acknowledge Moses' concern about his worthiness. Perhaps that is because his concern is out of focus, off the mark. Responding to God is not about one's worthiness at all—at least not as human beings measure worth.

How does your own sense of worth sometimes interfere with listening to God or sensing God's plan in your life? And when others indicate they feel unworthy to serve God in some way, how do you respond?

Instead, God makes a promise and offers a sign: "I will be with you." God's accompanying presence in Moses' life and in the life of the Hebrew people is what is most needed. God's guiding presence will lead them to the mountain where they will be given the words of the covenant to guide their lives into the future. This sign is to be an assurance to Moses. But Moses is still not quite so sure.

13"But," said Moses to God, "if I go to the Israelites and say to them, 'The God of your ancestors has sent me to you,' and they ask me, 'What is his name?' what do I tell them?" 14God replied to Moses: I am who I am. Then he added: This is what you will tell the Israelites: I AM has sent me to you. . . .

18They will listen to you. Then you and the elders of Israel will go to the king of Egypt and say to him: The LORD, the God of the Hebrews, has come to meet us. So now, let us go a three days' journey in the wilderness to offer sacrifice to the LORD, our God. 19Yet I know that the king of Egypt will not allow you to go unless his hand is forced. 20So I will stretch out my hand and strike Egypt with all the wondrous deeds I will do in its midst. After that he will let you go. . . .

Moses has a second objection that could be stated like this: "What if the people will not accept my authority and want to know who sent me? What name will I give them? By whose authority can I come to them?"

On the most basic level, having someone's name is like using a calling card. It adds weight to one's own presence to bring along the name of someone else, especially someone respected and powerful. It adds a layer of authority. On a theological level, asking God to reveal the divine name is asking God to reveal his very self. It might be seen as rather presumptive to even ask such a thing, but God is not fazed by this request. "I am who am" (in Hebrew, *Yahweh* or YHWH) is both a revelation about God's nature and somewhat of a holding back, only because we cannot fully comprehend all that it might mean.

> *"God is the fullness of Being and of every perfection, without origin and without end. All creatures receive all that they are and have from him; but he alone is his very being, and he is of himself everything that he is."*
>
> —Catechism of the Catholic Church *213*

Being given a divine name that is at once revealing and mysterious reminds us that being in relationship with God is learning to embrace the truly mysterious, that which can be known but never fully. Volumes have been written about the divine name revealed to Moses. One suggestion that might be most helpful is to think of God as saying "I am faithfully God for you, Moses." And God will faithfully be God for the Hebrews, for the early church, and for all generations who are open to God's actions in our world. The sign that will accompany this revelation of God's name is the "wondrous deeds" referred to in Exodus 3:20, the plagues (described in detail in Exod 7–11).

How have you experienced God acting faithfully for you?

**4:1“But,” objected Moses, “suppose they do not
believe me or listen to me? For they may say,
‘The LORD did not appear to you.’ ” 2The LORD
said to him: What is in your hand? “A staff,” he
answered. 3God said: Throw it on the ground.
So he threw it on the ground and it became a
snake, and Moses backed away from it. 4Then
the LORD said to Moses: Now stretch out your
hand and take hold of its tail. So he stretched
out his hand and took hold of it, and it became
a staff in his hand. 5That is so they will believe
that the LORD, the God of their ancestors, the
God of Abraham, the God of Isaac, and the God
of Jacob, did appear to you. . . .**

When Moses objects a third time, he dips back into the well of unworthiness. Such feelings and talk of unworthiness usually limits one's ability to hear and respond to God or even to others around us. It becomes a barrier to truly listening and it conveniently takes us out of the running for being responsible for a larger mission.

Consider a time when you were called upon to do something that was not in your usual area of comfort. Did a fear of being unsuccessful play a role in how you responded or acted? How were you able to address that fear?

Perhaps Moses is also expressing the fear of being unsuccessful, even in convincing the Hebrews to believe him and trust him. While it might be a legitimate concern for Moses (and for many of us) when called upon to act in ways for which he is unprepared, God again offers an assurance—this time by allowing the staff Moses carried as a shepherd to become a serpent. The following verses also list the healing of his leprous hand and the ability to turn the water of the Nile River to blood. The purpose is “so that they will believe,” indicating not so much an intellectual belief but the ability to trust Moses and the God who sends him on their behalf. God, it appears, is willing to use elements that are rather "fantastic" in order to accomplish liberation.

These signs will also be used when later addressing Pharaoh. It is as if God is providing Moses a foretaste of how he may garner Pharaoh's attention so that the liberation of his people will be accomplished.

10Moses, however, said to the LORD, "If you please, my Lord, I have never been eloquent, neither in the past nor now that you have spoken to your servant; but I am slow of speech and tongue." 11The LORD said to him: Who gives one person speech? Who makes another mute or deaf, seeing or blind? Is it not I, the LORD? 12Now go, I will assist you in speaking and teach you what you are to say.

Surely the modern reader will find this objection almost comical. Moses has already been engaged in a full-throated conversation with the Master of the Universe—and yet he objects that he is not eloquent! He certainly hasn't appeared to be "slow of speech and tongue" thus far but, no doubt, he is nervous about this turn of events and about speaking in the royal court. On top of it all, the message he is to deliver is not one that will be welcomed by the pharaoh of Egypt.

Can you think of a time when you saw a human weakness put to use to forward some aspect of God's plan?

Perhaps Moses' speech is a problem, but perhaps he is only floundering for another excuse that will take him out of the running for this job. In either case, God assures him that he is capable of handling whatever problems there might be. God will assist Moses and teach him what to say. This is another sign that God is willing to deal with the realities of human situations; God is committed to working through even human insecurities and deficiencies.

13But he said, "If you please, my Lord, send some-
one else!" 14Then the LORD became angry with
Moses and said: I know there is your brother,
Aaron the Levite, who is a good speaker; even
now he is on his way to meet you. When he sees
you, he will truly be glad. 15You will speak to him
and put the words in his mouth. I will assist both
you and him in speaking and teach you both
what you are to do. 16He will speak to the people
for you: he will be your spokesman, and you will
be as God to him. 17Take this staff in your hand;
with it you are to perform the signs.

And now we come to the heart of the matter: Moses simply does not want to do it. "Send someone else." There is a big difference between "I cannot" and "I will not." Up to this point, his objections have been centered on his abilities and insecurities, but now we arrive at an objection that is rooted in the will of Moses. And now the biblical storyteller reveals that God is angry and will put a stop to these protests and excuses. God still manages to take seriously the objection, so Moses is given the assistance of his own brother, Aaron, and both of them will be taught by God what to do.

The final line—"take this staff in your hand: with it you are to perform the signs"—tells Moses (and us) that the conversation is ending and the action is set to begin. This is a divine commission, and it will not be delayed or thwarted. God is the guarantor of its success, and Moses will be the instrument that God uses, even with his hesitations and insecurities. He has been well equipped for the liberating task before him, the freedom of God's people.

Whatever your burning bush experiences might be, have you found that surrendering to God ultimately gives you more freedom? Freedom from a personal agenda? Freedom from the fear of failure? Freedom to trust in God more deeply?

Some lessons that might be pondered for our own lives could include the following:

- When you are in pain and it is a result of injustice (as was the situation of the slaves), be sure to let God know about it. This can become an avenue of healing.
- When you see others hurting, God will not allow you to sit by comfortably, but will send you to go and to do.
- God is the one who is worthy. God equips us, and in the process of using that equipment we discover that our worthiness is measured in fidelity, not accomplishment.
- God is not an uninterested observer but is actively engaged in our world. Surprise of all surprises, God acts through us.
- When you discover that God has found you and called you, you will no doubt discover who you are in a most profound way.

What other lessons would you add to the list on page 37?

When God grabbed Moses' attention, it was not simply to awe him—God gave him a mission and gave him courage. God transformed him not simply for his own sake but for the sake of others. The burning bush in the wilderness allowed Moses to discover a world where the great I AM would offer liberation in place of enslavement and mutual love in place of cowering fear.

Praying the Word / Sacred Reading

One of the most profound divine promises in the entire Bible is God's statement to Moses: "I will be with you." This promise is repeated throughout the Bible in direct and indirect ways, and it is the very foundation for developing a trusting mutual relationship between ourselves and God. It is the reason that "Be not afraid" is also one of the most consistently used assurances throughout the Bible. God's very real presence with us allows us to operate from a place of trust rather than a place of fear. The following reflection might be a useful way to prayerfully ponder this reality.

> Every sign you offered to Moses, O God, was a demonstration of the promise to be with him as he moved forward into trusting your plan. "I will be with you" would come in the courage to rally his fellow Hebrews, in the authority he carried in knowing your name, in the abilities to use nature to capture attention, in the instruction to speak words of liberation, in the assistance of his brother.

I rejoice in knowing that you are with me as well, and that your presence in my life can be found in both ordinary and extraordinary ways. Teach me to step out in trust as I try to respond to your call in my life. Give me the assurances I need so that my response to your call can be transformative in our world.

You could just as easily say to me, O God, "I have been with you." Moses could review his life and know that your presence was with him when the midwives spared his life, when his mother created a watertight crib of sorts to float him in the Nile, when the Egyptian princess heard his cries and took him in, when even after a murderous response to evil he found protection in Midian and created a family there, when he was given a job to shepherd the flock of sheep whose needs led him to that burning bush.

I marvel in reviewing my life and finding evidence of your guiding, saving, protecting, and encouraging presence. May the evidence of your past interventions on my behalf and your past ability to stay with me in times of doubt give me the courage to search for your presence throughout each day and to rely on your steadfast love.

"I am with you" is the ever-present reminder that it is through God's presence in our lives that we are gifted and equipped to

live each day in service. Moses was called to bring the good news of liberation to a people oppressed by slavery. His call took them into a wilderness experience that gave them the covenant but also exposed their insecurities. In their wandering toward the Promised Land, it was that daily presence of God—a pillar of fire by night and of cloud by day, the gift of the Law, the traveling tabernacle of God's presence with them—that eventually led them to embrace a new identity as God's very own.

May your constant presence in the ever-present now, O God, give me the desire to continue to respond to your promptings in my life. Open my eyes to bushes that may be on fire. Open my ears to hear your voice. Open my mouth to respond, "Here I am." Open my will so that my desire to serve does indeed lead to action.

Living the Word

How will we make use of the ways God is equipping us for mission in the world?

- Could you take a step this week to see where your gifts might be needed in your neighborhood or in your parish? What new effort might you make to show your reliance on God's presence within you?
- Talk to a friend about an experience you have had of feeling God's call in your life. Perhaps by sharing even a simple story you

may help someone else look for evidence of God reaching out to them too.

- Make a conscious effort to learn about a situation of oppression in our world. Ask God to use your growing familiarity with this situation to work some good toward alleviating that pain.

The Exodus
EXODUS ROUTE
ALTERNATE EXODUS ROUTE
0 50 Miles
0 50 Kilometers
LUCIDITY INFORMATION DESIGN, LLC
The Great Sea
Sea of Reeds
Rameses
Succoth
GOSHEN
Heliopolis
Memphis
Heracleopolis
EGYPT
River Nile
EXODUS ROUTE
Red Sea
WILDERNESS OF SHUR
ALTERNATE EXODUS ROUTE
Brook of Egypt
SINAI
Dophkah?
Mt. Sinai
WILDERNESS OF PARAN
Kadesh-barnea
WILDERNESS OF ZIN
THE NEGEB
Gulf of Aqaba
Ezion-geber
MIDIAN
EDOM
Punon
Oboth
MOAB
Dibon
Mt. Nebo
Jericho
SALT SEA
Juttah
Arad
Hebron
Jerusalem
Ai
Bethel
CANAAN
Debir
Lachish
Beer-sheba
PLAIN OF PHILISTIA
Ashdod
Gaza